PUBLISHED BY HAVE IT ALL PRESS

Copyright © 2023 by Devin Alexander, Inc.

Published in the United States by Have It All Press, Los Angeles, a division of Devin Alexander, Inc.
www.devinalexander.com

HAVE IT ALL PRESS and its logo, are trademarks of Devin Alexander, Inc.

Book design by Michelle Pederson

Library of Congress Cataloging-in-Publication Data
Names: Alexander, Devin, 2023, author. | Pederson, Michelle, 2023, illustrator.
Title: Land of Secret Superpowers: Vegetables / by Devin Alexander; Illustrated by Michelle Pederson
Los Angeles, CA
Summary: Kids are enticed to eat vegetables when they learn the "Superpowers"
they'll likely gain when they do.
1. Children's Fiction 2. Nutrition 3. Diet Fitness

ISBN 978-1-7364569-0-3 (hardcover)

PRINTED IN CHINA
First Edition

Also by Devin Alexander:

You Can Have It!

The Most Decadent Diet Ever!

The Biggest Loser Cookbook

The Biggest Loser Dessert Cookbook

The Biggest Loser Family Cookbook

The Biggest Loser Quick and Easy Cookbook

The Biggest Loser Flavors of the World Cookbook

I Can't Believe It's Not Fattening!

Fast Food Fix

This book is dedicated to

my little veggie-eating angel.

You are the light of my life

and the life of the kitchen and beyond.

Thank you for "finding me."

The Land of Secret Superpowers: Vegetables

Written by
Devin Alexander

Illustrations by
Michelle Pederson

Have It All PRESS

Los Angeles

Every little girl and boy eats numerous times per day.

Without food, you'd never be able to jump, run, or play.

But did you know that some foods give you superpowers

while others can make you feel yucky and tired for hours?

There are foods that can make you grow big and strong.
There are foods that will give you energy to play all day long.
There are even foods that will help you run at such a fast pace,
you might even be able to beat your parents in a race.

There are foods that will help keep you feeling young.

And they'll create happiness on your tongue.

So turn these pages and pay close attention.

You're about to learn the secrets that so many people don't even mention.

Avocados

Aidan Avocado is one energetic guy!

He can run fast and jump high.

Eat avocados today,

and you'll be ready to go out and play!

Beets

Brian Beet is the best at sports!
So, eat some beets if you want to
rule the baseball, basketball,
or tennis courts.

Broccoli

Bella Broccoli has been known
to improve your mood.
So eat some broccoli,
and you could become a cool dude.

Carrots

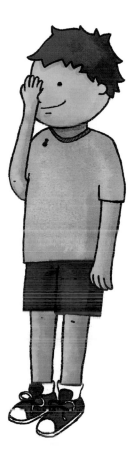

Cayenne Carrot has perfect eyesight.

Even at night, she barely needs a flashlight.

Eat some carrots, and you will see

just how strong your eyes will be.

Celery

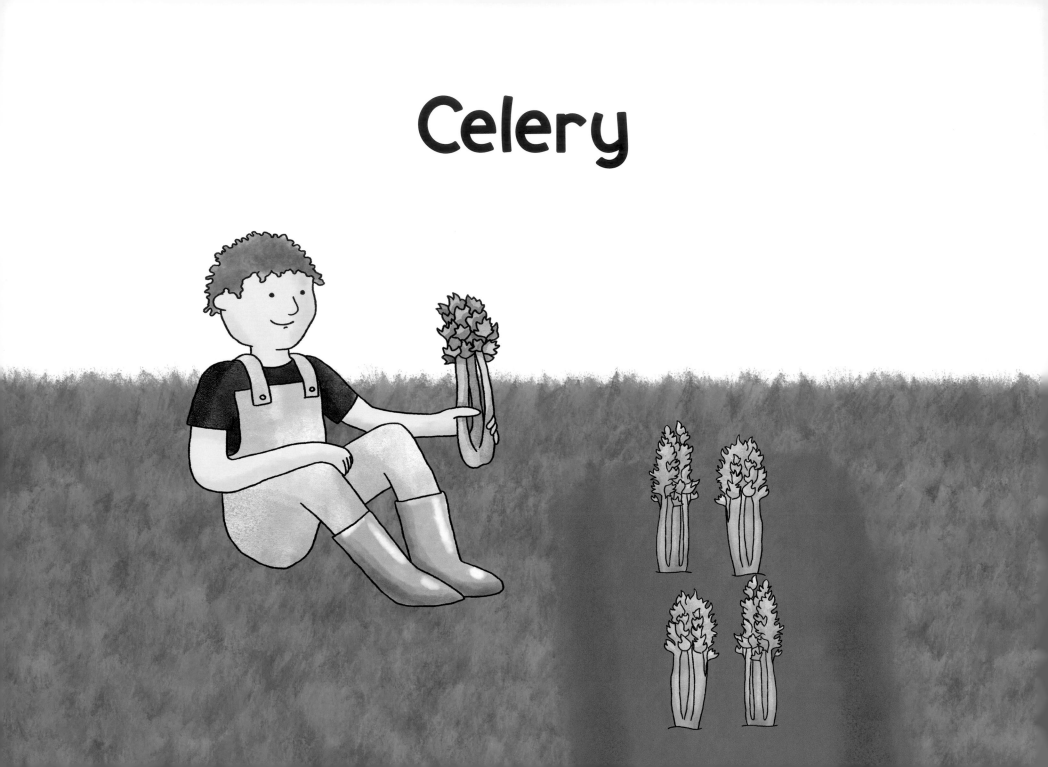

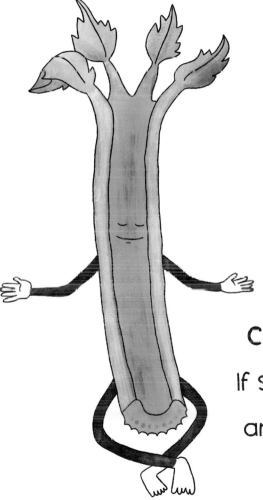

Charlotte Celery keeps you calm. If something scares you, eat celery and get an extra hug from mom.

Kale

Kaylee Kale can get a cut,

and a scab will form to close it shut.

So be sure to add kale to your plate,

and healing any wounds will be your fate.

Mushrooms

Mason Mushroom feels just great!

He's always in a perky state.

If you are in a sluggish mood,

mushrooms might be the perfect food.

Potatoes

Patrick Potato performs much more
powerfully than most!
Eat some potatoes,
and your body and brain will
work well from coast to coast.

Red Bell Peppers

Riley Red Pepper can bask in the sun
and be more protected while having fun.
Sunburns won't run to you if you eat red bell peppers
and use sunscreen too!

Spinach

Savannah Spinach is super strong.

She can lift things all day long.

Want to carry heavy things and throw far?

Eat some spinach,

and you could end up being a track star.

Sweet Potatoes

Scarlett Sweet Potato can run for hours

and dance all night long.

Eat sweet potatoes, and you'll want

the DJ to play song after song

after song!

Squash

Skylar Squash can hold her breath

for a really long time;

her powerful lungs keep her at her prime.

When squash is a veggie you eat,

you might even become a world-class athlete!

Tomatoes

Trevor Tomato can do a nifty trick.

Turning green to red so quick.

Eat tomatoes summer, spring,

winter, and fall;

you'll have strong bones

and you'll be able to grow tall.

So now you know some foods that are best to eat.

Eat them all raw or cook them over heat.

Whatever you do, remember one thing.

If you eat enough veggies, you'll feel amazing!

About the Author
Devin Alexander

The Land of Secret Superpowers: Vegetables is from *New York Times* bestselling author and celebrity chef, Devin Alexander. She has maintained a 70-pound weight loss and helped thousands of moms (of the pickiest kids!) end exhaustive mealtime battles. Devin thought she hated vegetables half of her life and then realized that they were always just "marketed" wrong to her. When she became a mom, she was committed to doing what it takes to make sure her daughter eats in a healthy way. This book is the latest step in their journey.

www.FitMomFitKids.com

www.DevinAlexander.com

To the SUPER Adult reading this:

Obviously, eating one leaf of spinach is not going to make you strong, and a nibble of a carrot won't make you see better. This book is designed to get kids excited about eating vegetables, as it's a proven fact that eating a healthy diet including fruits and vegetables generally keeps us healthier and happier.

That said, Devin Alexander is not a dietitian or doctor. Always seek advice from your pediatrician before incorporating any new foods into your child's diet.

Fun Facts For Parent & Child:

Though the tomato is technically a fruit, in 1983, the Supreme Court of the United States ruled that the tomato must be considered a vegetable since it's most commonly eaten as a vegetable.

Some of the other "vegetables" that are actually fruit, to many people's surprise, include: avocados, beans, butternut squash, chickpeas, corn, cucumber, eggplant, okra, peas, peppers, pumpkin, string beans, and zucchini.

Avocados help me
run fast

Beets help me
jump high

Broccoli makes me
feel happy

Carrots help
me see

Celery keeps
me calm

Kale makes my
boo-boos go away